Black August

EL SHABAZZ

Black August

Copyright 2018 EL-SHABAZZ

Royal Falcon Publishing, Palmdale, CA 93550
Printed in the United States

ISBN-13: 978-1726472340
ISBN-10: 1726472345

Printed by Createspace 2018
Published by Royal Falcon 2018

Website: Royalfalconpublishing.com
Contact: Royalfalconpublishing@gmail.com

Dedicated to The Children of The Sun

ONCE MEN

YES, There were Once Men in This World,
Who gave Clothes, Shelter, Medical Attention and Free
Breakfast to our
Boys and Girls,
They Existed in Communal Social Constructs of Caring for
Self and
Kind,
A Courageous and Selfless Breed, who met the Aspirations
and Needs of a People who had been stripped of their Dignity
and
Pride,
They were a Beautiful Bunch, who were in a Rush to Freedom,
Justice and Self
Defense,
Blessed with Common Sense, Caught up in some Crazy Shyt,
From the Stock of Slaveships, Auctioned off into Slavery by a
Racist and Capitalist
White Government,
They were Uncovering The Conspiracies and Hidden
Histories, While unlocking The Soul of Black Power
Energy,
They came to Right The Wrongs, and Write the Songs for a
Liberation Brawl that Oppressed The People under Criminal
Laws,
The Pigs of Disorder, Brought Terror to the Black Quarters,
The Brutal Nature of Those Less than Animals, were Black
Body
Poachers,
Snakes and Vultures, The Children of Slave Owners in
possession of Stolen Property,

Black August

The Guilt in the Filth, The Cold Northerners have made things
Colder,
But These Brave Men Rose to The Occasion,
In The Interest of the Black Nation,
This was No Time for Waiting,
Freedom has No Patience,
Black Love is Conquering Self Hating,
They were The Vanguard, Setting The Bar
With Visions into the Far,
Sankofa, They were Looking Back Forward to be Exactly Who
They Are,
But The Die was Set, Through a Counter Intelligence Program,
infiltration of Informants and Terror Squad Forces,
Murdered, Slaughtered and Shot Up,
Those they didn't Kill they Locked Up,
And The Beautifully Strong Black Women who Stood with
them, were
Murdered, Slaughtered and Shot Up,
Those they didn't Kill they Locked Up,
And We are The Children of Those,
So What Stops Us,
With Strange Names like HUEY, FRED, STOKELY, BUNCHY
AND GEORGE,
They Opened Up The Door to REVOLUTION,
POWER TO THE PEOPLE,
FOOD, CLOTHING AND SHELTER TO THE POOR...
YES... THERE WERE ONCE MEN IN THIS
WORLD,
and THIS WE SHOULD TELL TO OUR BOYS AND GIRLS...

HOW FLY IS YOUR LOVE?

My love is as fly as the 70's , bell bottomed out, with Butterfly collars,
I got that smooth cognac Billy Dee Williams Mahogany Love, that makes you wanna Holla,
I'm like your grandmommas peach cobbler driving down the street in a 1972 Glasshouse Impala,
Curtis Mayfield in the 8 track ' The Makings of You ' because I'm ' So In Love ' I wanna repaint the sky a brighter blue,
I'm like the Rufus to your Chaka Khan, ' Tell Me Something Good'.. ' Sweet Thing '
I'm like that Soul Train Line, Groovin' up your Thighs, putting monkey bites on your neck, while doing the Electric slide, or we can take it back to the Grapevine,
I got that Richard Pryor tickle you to your funny bone, Square Biz, No Jiving, I dig the Funk in your step, I'm like Nixon trying to tap into your phone,
I'm that five on the black hand side, lets take a midnight drive across the flashlight sky, like it's December 31st , 1979,
Don't miss that Mothership connection, I like them Mother Hips and Blessings,
Them Lady Sing the Blues eye Lashes, I keep it outta sight, because my Good Times are so Dyno-mite!
I can make you shake your groove thang, over a bowl of Peaches and Herb,
My love is like Summertime fire hydrant water blasting off the curb ,
I'm like that Sta Sof Fro in your Afro Puffs, putting glittering stars in your Natural,
I'll hug you like Hott pants, and have you walking tall like platforms, I'm that Kool, with a Black Fist in my Afro,

Black August

My love is socially conscious and anti-war, I'm like a Black
Panther feeding the children and defending the poor,
Everybody can have a little if some people stop taking more,
Ain't no thang but a chicken wang, I'm taking my Lady to the
Drive In for a double feature , The Mack and The Spook who
sat by the Door,
I'm that 45, B-Side Love Song that lovers dance to in their
living room, after putting the children to bed, for the night is
young for dancing tongues, happy hands and caressing hugs,
lip crawling to tickle your fancy,
hip gripping and back scratching, deep diving and finger
licking as you moan... Oohhh you sooo Nasty....
And as I drench your wings soaking wet, Now answer me
this...How Fly is your Love?

THEM IS YOU

I know this Chocolate Sister, like two Big scoops of double
fudge Brownie cakes ,
like Oh My Yummie Goodness ,
Shouldn't this ,
Be plastered all over the globe,
From her High charged Beautiful Black Antennas,
To the Chocolate puddles at her toes,
Gotta fierce Walk, like puttin pot holes in my lawn,
She's the crack before dawn, the Blackest Part of the Light,
Can't even look at her lips without wanting to take a bite,
She got that good vibe,
Sister Soul, you can't hurt her with no sticks and stones,
and Names, you'll call her Queen, even after you know her
name,
Grooving her Hips under a dancing wind blown sun dress,
without a lick of Shame,
From a pair of scrubs, to Dashikis and Hijabs or them jeans
and Boots That you make look Oh so Cute,...

I know this Coco Brown Sister, like roasted Carmel over candy
apples, sweet like that Cinnamon toast church ,
And she got that street touch, like late night on my arms
stilettos or just hangin at the basketball courts in a pair of
Chucks,
Butterflies and Tiger claws tattooed, cause she's a Beautiful
Wild Cat, hear her Roar as I make her Purrrrr,
In her twist and curves,
Damn right their hers,
She melt my words like hot butter syrup,

Black August

And scoop me up like brown sugar cubes dropped in her sun
roasted coffee swirl ,
Ride or Die type, like Tupac saying Me and My Girlfriend
against the World,...

I know This RedBone Sister, Like honeycomb Sunshine
I call her Shea Butter Gold,
She's creamy butterscotch melting on your tongue like your
childhood memories ,
She map the constellations while eating sun drops and yellow
moon pies with explosions of delightful energy,
Like canary diamonds powered on flesh and bone that
Kathleen cleaver fever under bright black sun-rays,
With a lemon squeeze of attitude cause she's just as Black as
you,
Hand on her hip and fist in your lip if you talk shit,
we stick together like chocolate peanut-butter reese's cups,
She go , hair laid, braids or locks, fresh to def, you got my
number, and when you call,
I'll pick up,

I got a taste for Chocolate, Cinnamon and Butterscotch with a
Big Bowl of
Passionfruit ,
Just some Sisters I know,..
But I bet one of
Them is You...

Black August

First World Temple
Sermon # 7

Children of the Sun,
I Send you Greetings from the Moon Mother Glorious
who looks over your nightly ensembles with the Dream Dance
melodies of consciousness pressed into your Sweet Souls like
grapes and passion fruit ,
The Root of Abraham grows deeper than Adam,
The Mother of Eve is the 7th generation Granddaughter of The
First World Women who Dreamed up
Man....

I was sent as their Poet Prophet to trumpet glad tidings of the
7th world birth which is swimming in the wombs of the 6th
world women,
Who thought their troubles would never end and carried the
tears of their world on their shoulders which made for heavy
cries that buckled their bellies with agonizing whys , they
were brutally oppressed and chained to the wicked land of the
wasted,
tucked in the shadows of men who feared their light with the
romantic swindle of candlelit dinners to hide their dark
intentions
in the phantom fantasies of felonious fools
and
they still held to the gut belief that their world would birth a
True
Man....

Ready your Wombs Women,

Black August

The seed has been dropped and your screams have been heard
from the wailing of crushed souls
who
sung a song so sad it would make a brass monkey cry ,
Blessed are the thighs that spread the future wide open for the
Promise Child,
an immaculate expression of Love and a 7th World Mercy
burping
coconut
breast milk,
so gather around Women, let your dresses down
or
Stand your hair up
for the Jubilee Celebration is in full swing
and
I'm just here to give you a push that your feet may tickle the
sky a brighter blue like out of spring water baptism for onto
us
a Son is Born...
Man....

WHO SHOT MALCOLM

Who Shot Malcolm ?
Trayvon ain't Talkin',
Emmett got Pictures,
Oscars Murder Mantra,
Mourning Wombs,
Our Mama's Pain,
Birthing Answers,
Caught'um on Camera,
Climbing the Wall
with Jacob's Ladder,
Kill My Future,
Assassins Creed,
Bleed Ni##a Bleed,
They Slept Our King
for having Dreams,
Nat Turners Revenge
and
Rosemary's
Blue Eyed Devil
Baby
Is Looking for
Assata in a
Cuban
Crisis,
With Isis Papers
Rolling a Joint,
Fukc A-Rab Money,
We Got Blood
Money,
So what's the

Black August

Point,
in talking Slick like Oil,
Somebody Got Paid
For Killing
Malcolm X,
and Now They
Living
Royals,
Just ask Lorde,
Malcolm told the white girl she can't join it,
But she can support it,
Spy VS Spy,
Too Many Ni##as got
Green Eyes,
Not all the Shooters had on
Bow Ties,
We Buried Malcolm Facing
Mecca,
And Y'all gonna have to Face
Allah,
El-Raheem, The Merciful,
Just don't let The
Muslims
Catch'cha...
Who Shot Malcolm?
Trayvon ain't Talkin',
Emmett got Pictures,
Oscars Murder Mantra,
Like
We
got Answers
For these
Mama's...

Unbeknownst to Herself

She was Beautiful for Reasons
Unbeknownst to Herself,
Like a Cosmic Swan dipped in
Black Pearl and Volcanic
Earth,
Her People were Polished in Diamond
In a Long Line of Prophets from
Eden to Mecca, Speculations and Logic
and Kisses that lead to
Birth,
She was a Blue Bone, Homegrown like
A Pot of Soul, She goes Good with
Vegetables and Hot Buttered Rolls,
Curled Toes and Angelic Moans,
She was just the Quench for my
Thirst,
If Black Don't Crack, She was Marbled in
Youth, She had Girl in her Eyes and Woman in her Thighs,
Beauty at her Root with a
Tongue fit for Truth, that was
preoccupied with
I Love You, Only I Said it
First,
She was Beautiful for Reasons
Unbeknownst to Herself,
Like Yesterday and Forever,
And it just so Happens,
She always remembers to Cover Her
Worth….

SOMALI BUTTERFLY

I Crushed a Sweet Little Somali Butterfly
Acting Cute and Playing Pretty
She was born in the Garden but
Raised in the
City,
She got Rug Burns from Prayers
And Shea Butter Conversations to
Smooth over the Harsh Reality of
A Beautiful Lie with the Sky Blue Ugly
Truth ....
Oh Really???
She's so Picky, after Tupac Died, She stopped listening to
Biggie,
I don't know how she remembers that
Because she was so Itty Bitty,
Just around the size of a Penny,
But She was that Loyal that her
Devotion was never
Iffy,
She had her Contradictions like Lipstick and
Eye Shadow as if She really needed that,
She was Yellow Black with Blue Bone
Roots, Yemen Branches and a Lap fit for
Persian
Kitties,
Kissy Kissy, I Feel like The Arabian Prince singing Darling
Little Prissy, I must be Dreaming, I mean what was I Thinking,
Crushing a Somali Butterfly
Like things wouldn't get
Sticky....

AFRIKA'S HUSBAND

Afrika is the Woman I Love but America is the B!tch I'm with,
And I'm trying to get out this destructive relationship, she's
into chains and whips and all kinds of freaky shit,
The whore stands in the ports of New York, holding a torch
because she's a woman of the night with a tongue like a fork,
With her sneaky lying ass calling herself Liberty with Slavery
tattooed on her left Titty,
Attitude always shitty, everything about her is Iffy, she's
known as slum pu$$y in every urban city,
And talk about a thief, the b!tch stole me from my Woman
Afrika, took all my Gold and Diamonds,
buried my history, changed my name and made me worship
her pagan god and lynching my ass for even trying,
to break free and speak truth, she took me to court and threw
me in jail,
Knowing damn well I don't have money for bail so she gave
me her drugs to sell, lifted up her skirt and told me to inhale
the smell,
B!tch your shit stank , dripping with syphilis and Aids, telling
everybody we engaged, you put a nigga in your outhouse to
sucker my vote, slavery by another name,
But Marcus Garvey delivered me a message from Afrika My
Woman,
She said she is awaiting the return of her Husband, and that I
should hurry Home, because strange men are at her doors,
with d!cks and greed in their hands,
Unzipping their pants, with violence and rape drooling from
their mouths, she said she will fight as best as she can, but to
get the upper hand she is going to need her Man,

Black August

Our Children are starving, the brave men are dead and unborn,

and her beautiful dress was torn in war to get to the Peace between her thighs and in her heart she swore,

To resist all rape attempts even if they blacken her eyes and bust her lips, they will never enjoy the glory of Afrika's Hips,

She said the black face leaders are nothing more than puppets with foreign hands jammed far up their asses,

Allowing other lesser men to make passes, crashing on her couch, while she's looking for a Machete to start slashing- ouch!

Hurry home my Love , I sealed this message in blood, rescue your kisses and hugs , that we may fly free again like the falcon and dove,

I tucked her letter deep in the pockets of my soul,

Rolling out of Americas satin sheet whorish bed , slipping back into my clothes,

I'm dressed in Red Black and Green, and this B!tch got the nerves to Scream,

Talking about I thought we were a team,... snap out of that dream you trying to kill me like Martin Luther King ,

Don't you see this soul ring on my finger, I belong to Afrika , the Woman you stole me from,

You want me for sex, sport and play, my happiness is with Afrika, you just want to make me gay, at your banquet table begging for crumbs,

To my Beloved Afrika, I am on my way, through my stumble, fall and crawl,

I will lift myself up and put my back against the wall because After all,

We have a love story to continue and more gardens to plant from the lovers balcony,

Black August

we will seed the world with Peace and Harmony as you smile
on my kisses you are so proud of me,
I left the lust of a whore for the Love of a Woman,
and we will reNew our vows before the families of the world
as I Love, Respect and Protect you as Afrika's Husband...

BLUE BONE

Blue Bone,
Gold Blooded,
Silk Threaded,
She's So Soul, Rhythm & Choice,
Time Immemorial, Epic Aeons and Water Echoes, with Lotus
Ponds sitting on Her
Voice,
Blue Grass Melodies over Coltrane back tracks, Symphonies of
Yesterday's
Tomorrow,
Swivel Swans Swinging Swaying back and forth like
Nectarines dancing in the
trees, 12 Midnights under Purple Rain, Fire and
Charcoal,
Blue Moon, Silver Clouds and Cursive Eyelashes, Crushed
Earth and Soft Curved Culture,
Lips of Jupiter Soaked in Ruby Wells with the Best of Wishes
and
Kisses,
Organic Royal, Sweet Saturated Soil, Her Root Runs Wildly
Skin Deep, Squeeze and Pop Goosebumps just to Feel Her
Feathers Drenched in Sky,
Sweet as Bean Pie
and
Black as
Afrikan Cultivated
Licorice,...
I Call Her
Blue Bone....

BLACK AMERICAN MUSLIM

Islam came to America in the Bowels of Slave Ships,
European
Enterprise,
Human Trafficking,
Hostages,
Kidnapped Victims ,
and The Horrors of Rape, Ravaged
Black
Thighs,
In the Chains of Spain, this is Get back from when the Moors
Reigned, turning Tables with slave cables, unable to Break
Free, This is New World
Happening,
The Gold Coast is the Slave Post, Troubled waters, and Rock-
a-Bye Boats, Portugal's Criminals came for the Best Stock of
Afrikans,
What'cha Thinking England ain't gonna come in Here
Swinging, Bringing The Worse Terror ever known to Man,
Drunken Murderers ,
Stolen Wealth and Labor,
Christians Right ???
Do unto your
Neighbors....???
Don't Do Us No Favors,
Keep your fake white Christ,
We already know Jesus was one of us,
But None of Us,
Made it an issues,
Until you started fukcin with All of Us,
Now they Hauling Us,

Black August

And When they Heard us
Calling Up...
ALLAHU AKBAR!!!'
They like Aww Hell Naww,
We ain't gonna Let it go that
Far,
So They Murdered our Parents,
So they could be our Teachers,
Murdered our Imams,
And they became our Preachers,
Outlawed our Quran's ,
and turned us into Bible Readers,
We were at the Top of Civilization,
Now we're Bottom
Feeders,
They Destroyed our Culture, Language, Religion and
Names ,
Now we Apple Pie, English Speaking, Southern Baptist,
And Jamal is now known as
James,
But Don't Trip,
I'm coming Back for my
Stolen Goods,
Thanks to Duse', Ali, Fard, Elijah and Ahmad,
I found a Masjid in my Neighborhood,
Malcolm, Louis and Wallace,
Told me the Best example of Human Excellence ,
with All Due Respect to Momma,
Is The Prophet
Muhammad,
So when y'all wanna Talk about Freedom and
Independence,
Talk to a Black American Muslim,

Black August

Who never gave up the birthright of Afrika or Islam,
With Peace as
The
Eternal
Mission…..

WHO YOU BE

Like a Chocolate Pearl with a Polishing Smile,
Her Beauty was Effortless, Black Lotus on the Skin of the
Blue Nile,
Sun Soaked like an Apricot Morning,
Freshly Blushed,
Cashmere to the Touch, as if to say what if Angels were
One of Us,
Like saying She's Beautiful,
just ain't Enough,
If Heaven had a height, She would raise it Up,
Beyond Spoken Word, and Hypersensitive Verbs, There's not
even a Language for
Her,
They say she speaks in the dialect of Birds, things we never
heard, like out of the Sky Blue, She Flew into her own Lip
Curves ,
Blissful and Blessed, like Happy and Yes, Winter Peppermint
Breath, with Eastern Fabrics Gracing her
Neck,
Like a mirror with a glimpse, What you see is what you Get,
and So much more than you expect or even could Accept,
She said Peace Earthlings, We're Khalifah Supremes, The Light
Breathes, it knocks you to your Knees, like Oh Good Lord
Please,
Mercy Me, they ain't gonna Worry Me, Her Smile was a
Courtesy, from the Heart of Generosity ,
She had one Policy,
All things are Honesty,
Ain't No Hiding from
Who

Black August

You Be …

DONT SHOOT?

I'm as Black and Proud as Mike Brown
Getting Shot Down,
As My People Stand Around,
and Watch this Pig Slaughter
Me in Full Camera View,
If it were You,
I would've Pick up a Clip, a Fist, a Kick, a Brick, a Toothpick
or even just
Spit,
But Damn It, I would've did some Sh!t,
To let that Pig know We ain't with that
Sh!t!!!
Put your Damn Hands Down and Stop Saying
DONT SHOOT,
If you gonna Riot and Loot, at least hit the Gun Shop, and get
a Bazooka, a Pistol Grip Pump, some 9's and 45's,
Fukc it, give me a Slingshot and a
22'
But y'all gonna Stop Fukcin wit Us,
This a New Breed, With No King and No Dream,
We the Cousins of Trayvon and Oscar Grant, but Gangsta Rap
won't even Shoot Back,
So just leave it to a
Poet to
Rant,
But after all that,
We gotta hit the Basement
And Start Organizing
Blacks,

Black August

and I ain't said
Sh!t
Til
We Shoot Back ...

The Hon. Marcus Garvey - "The Call"

First Son of Afrika, Proudly and Courageously you stood for
The Highest Principles of the Soul,
Bold and Forthright, You Proclaimed Our Manhood, Our
Womanhood and Our Nationhood and paved our Road,
Out of the primordial rich Blackness of Culture and Faith you
dedicated yourself to Our People,
A life of sacrifice and service, you stood Strong, exceptionally
Grand and Regal,
From an island to The World you herald The Coming of an
Afrikan World and Empire,
You lifted us High on your Shoulders that We may vision the
world through the eyes of a Giant as you
Inspired,
You took us out of slavery into Freedom, Oh Black Moses,
Great Liberator you broke through the impossible,
You fashioned us into Men and Women, Through Love and
Discipline, you are a Gentleman of the Highest creed, Devoted
and Honorable,
You took us out of the Slums into a Community , out of
division and ignorance, into Knowledge and Unity, you took
us out of sharecropping into People of Commerce and
Business, from the Dumb Deaf and Blind to a People of
Creativity and Vision,
You gave us the Arts and The Science of Civilization, You
made Black more Beautiful and Turned us into a Nation,
Oh Elegant Black Poet light the fires of our Passions with your
Words Romancing our People into a Dance with destiny,
To the Sound of Afrikan Drums, We catch the rhythm in our
Hips and Soul for you gave me the Best in Me,

Black August

The Rest of Me is playing Catch Up in The Marching Band of
your Black Legionnaires ,
We are a People of Valor and Resolve, from Dance and Song,
to Chemist and Engineers,
Men and Women of Great Affair, Out of The Enriched Black
Soil of Royal Blood This Timeless People are Pressing on ,
Thanks to you Mr. Marcus Garvey, who gave us Lessons
shown,
You gave us Respect, Pride and Responsibility , to the meeting
Halls of Liberty,
The Black Star Line enterprise , you brought us Freedom-
Ships, The only Black Man to Sail us Back to Afrika through
his own Energy,
And Those of US who multiplied The Drive for Independence,
You Gave us a Flag and an Anthem , A Place under the Sun
and Beautified our Image,
The Red Black and Green is The Whirlwind through which the
suffering millions will Triumph
One God, One Aim, One Destiny and Nothing will Divide us ,
From The Negro World to The Afrikan Communities League ,
We follow where you Lead because The Ancestors have
approved your Dream,
Through your Heart and Dedication , you have given us a
New Sun, a Brighter Future and The Blueprint to Freedom, We
became Peace Greeters and Readers, Our
Children Teachers and Leaders, Panthers Lions and Guerrillas,
Organic and Conscious and World Pillars,
We Salute you President General of The U.N.I.A., and The
New Afrikan World,
You made us into Black Diamonds and Black Pearls,
Beautifully in our Skin Through our Minds , Soaked in our
Souls , we carry the banner of service and sacrifice , A People
fashioned in Gold...

Black August

Afrika for The Afrikans at Home and Abroad,
The Voice that came from Liberty Hall, is Sounding through us
All...
Thank You President General Marcus Garvey for making The
Call...

THANK YOU SISTER

Sister, if I had my way with the world, Colored Girls would rainbow the sky , rain down kisses and foot their feet in clouds , their laughter would be music groovin us into parties of hip ensembles rich black tones of melody memories moving between Black Emeralds and Red Bones and all those roasted Brown Sugar fillings, that fills the imagination of feelings I haven't found words for,
from Los Angeles to Darfur and I got more Travels for I even heard they got you in Singapore ,..
Universal Mother of Civilization, pregnant belly full of Nations, a Woman's Worth is measured by what you Birth, Men have called you everything from Heaven to Earth, they're so confused by you, they want to strip you Naked and Cover you from Head to Toe, from Jesus Momma to Queen Nefertiti, and all the Hail Marys you can muster, to All the Betty's and Coretta's who make Great Men Better, I'm forever Indebted , and just read it in a scientific journal they found your East Afrikan Bones from 7 million years ago and even She had a Momma,.. So what I look like not paying Homage , when " Heaven lies at the Foot of Mother", these are the words of Prophet Muhammad...
Sister if I had my way with the world, Colored Girls would be a movie beyond Poetry, Pain and Heartbreak , I would Celebrate you like National Holidays, New Year Parades and the Newest Style of Braids that you figured through your fingers, your touch of creation even created all The Worlds Races,
You're the Start and Finish-line, Divine, Sublime and cheap men call you a Dime because they don't know how to mine for Diamonds, and Treasures of Heart, Soul and Mind,.. And Sure

you have your attitudes and moments , but they made you
shoulder the world between your Hips,.. You Suppose to
Trip,.. And still you wipe your tears and say,.. I Got This!!!

Thank You Sister'!!!

ONCE UPON THE SANDS OF TIME

Once upon the sands of time, existed a land flowing with Milk
and Honey,
Where rainbows would tickle the belly of the sky even making
the Sun laugh a brighter Sunny,
Laughter was the order of the day, singing and dancing was
the organic time clock of a timeless people,
Regal in Culture and favored by the Ancient of Days, their
natural religion was called Peaceful,
They positioned themselves perpendicular to the grand
waterfalls of Kush near the Eastern gates of Eden directly
under the pillars of Heaven and they counted everything by
Sevens,
In their land, Lions were the Shepherds of Sheep and their soil
was deliciously rich enough to eat, they would often snack on
rose petals and peppermint leaves, in the cool of a fine mist
with a dancing breeze,
In-between their conversations of song, music was their
language mathematically composed,
with sweet whispers in melody and timeless rhythm folds,
Their Women perfumed the air with their breath of jasmine
giggles, on hill tops they would pluck stars out of the sky for
the children to glitter themselves with and rest them on clouds
of pillows , nap time was a dream
Once lived through the eclipse of time raining through the
hour glass of cosmic journeys ...., these were a people in no
hurry ...
The Men would carve poetry into mountains as love notes to
their delightful darlings,
Dancing on the four winds of their hearts, their kisses would
spark smokeless flames called passion,

Black August

Dashing Men who fashion temples from their bodies,
impeccable infrastructure A work of art and soulfully Godly,
Their Women were of a clandestine Beauty like an angels
Secret face unveiled Through holiness at the neck lines of
grace, their lips were like peeled summer plums, bursting
juice pockets of sweetness with kisses that run down your
chin that you try to catch with your tongue,
They swallow kisses to make babies, bellies full of Suns and
Moons,
Giving birth at the 9th hour Because the Women bring home
the Breast of Food,
Milk and Honey is the diet of new born souls who burp the
future into existence ,
Untold worlds unfold on the belly side of baby fat kisses,
Once Upon the Sands of Time in the land of Lovers in Love,
existed the children of God, who lost their way but still Dream
of their time that always was.....

THE FINDINGS

I Questioned The
Elder,
What ever became of
that Great Black Race of
Monolithic,
Men of Principle and Women of Pinnacle, Architects of
Conscious Culture, Science, Civilizations and
Common
Sense,
He Replied,
They Forgot Their Histories,
Their Names and Their Lands,
Their Languages and Their Plans,
Their Manners and Their Chants,
Their Harvest and Their Plants,
Their Elephants and Their
Ants,
Their Drums and Their Dance,
And Traded Their Cans in for
Can't's,....
They gave way to Excuses,
And The Worst Forms of Abuses, and A Mangled Monkey
Mockery sad example of Music....
They Only Look like Us,
But They don't Cook Like Us,
They forgot what goes Goes Good with What,
and Word around these Parts, Many of them even Eat Pigs
Butt,
YUCK,

Black August

They were Hit Over the Head,
And Left for
Dead,
They had a Prophet who kept the Diet of
Fish and Bread,
But they leave them all out to Dry,
Like Strange Fruit on Southern Trees, Swinging Necks on
High,
Over 2,000 Seasons and Counting....
The Elder Said, Their Time Cometh Again,
Why you think we're Smiling,
Of All Places,
This is Where God has
Found Us,.....

BLACKBERRY SUNRISE

I had Good Reason to Believe She was born on a Saturn Birth
Cycle,
Shadowless Moons, under Black Falcon Fame, doused in the
rains of
Cairo,
Grew up on a Wheat Farm, Played in Milk Groves and Wore
Her Skin in
Raven Hues,
She was Branded Beauty on Glassless Beaches, Soaked her
Knees in Candied Peaches,
She was from a People Blacker than
Blue,
Shimmering Silvers, Metals made of Water, Paper Bright Skies,
She held the Future in Her Thighs,
I had Good Reason to Believe,
She Sat on a
Blackberry
Sunrise…

" NINAS OWN "

I'm the God Son of Nina Simone,
With Backlash in my Blue Bones,
I'm Malcolm Littles Cellmate,
I Went with Malik El Shabazz after the Break,
I'm Marcus Garvey's First Lieutenant,
The Black Star Lines First Passenger,
Black in Business,
I'm Elijah Muhammad's Star Minister
And Imam W.D. Mohammed's New Signature,
I'm Fred Hampton's Roommate,
And Bunchy Carters's Shiny
Black Thirty Eight,
I'm Maya Angelou's First Poem,
Tattooed on Nikki Giovanni's Yellow
Right Shoulder,
I'm Angela Davis Gap Tooth Smile,
And Huey P Newtons Black Panther Growl,
I'm the Bee Sting of Muhammad Ali,
And The H.Rap Brown of Howard University,
I'm Emmett Tills Last Dying Wish,
And Sarah Baartman's Unforgiving Hips,
I'm Tupac Shakur's Concrete Rose,
I Put A Spell On You
Like The Broken Heart of
Nina Simone...

BLACK MEANING

More Black Babies are Born on the Back End of a Back
Slap,
Stormy Black Eyes, Soul Sorrows Slowly Dripping out as
Black
Sap,
Black Child with a Black Cloud over its Black Brow,
And I don't care how Light Skin you are,
You're
Black Now,
Screaming Black Falcon Down,
Cheering for Somali's,
Black Ali,
Starving Black Bodies,
Black Mama's Crying Black Murder,
Black Herders,
From Black Zulu's
To
Black Berbers,
Black Workers and Black Servers, a Date Shake with a Black
Bean
Burger,
Could Feed a Black Village ,
in your white dreams,
Remember we said,
It's a Black Thing, you wouldn't understand ,
Like a Helping Black Hand
and a Black Woman who still
Cherish a
Black Man,
With Black Presidents from Afrika to America,

Black August

And these Black Characters on Black Entertainment Television
are the
Black Inheritors,
Of Harriet, Sojourner, Clara, Betty, Coretta, Rosa, and Your
Momma,
How could you
Embarrass Her,
Black Pride, Black Jive,
Black Power Salute and Give Me 5, on The
Black Hand Side,
Black Love don't get a shot because of a
Black Gun,
Black Fathers behind Black Bars, Black Daughters Stripping
for Dollars, Black Momma's in the middle of the Street, like
Black Madonna's Gripping Death, Soaked in Blood,
Sobbing to The World
Not My Black Son,
Black Natives and Black Saviors,
Black Lovers and Black
Haters,
Black Moses
and
Black Jesus,
Black Muhammad
The
Best Black
Kept
Secrets,
Black Achievements,
Black Failures for all the white reasons,
I'm just trying to give
The Truth
BLACK MEANING....

JUST AFTER DARK

I would love to dance with you on the bright side of a Nubian
moon under a crisp midnight Afrikan sky,
With a Mali drum beat vibe groovin' through your thighs,
filling up your soul and spilling out of your eyes,
Joyful tears bring rain which springs a garden oasis out of
Sahara sand,
As we ride on the backs of the Lions of Tanzania across the
stretch of the land,
Seeding the Earth with Love and Flowers , under the showers
of Blessings and Big Lip kisses while holding
Hands,
Diving into the Nile from the peaks of the pyramids as I swim
across your smile only to drown in our Forever Right Now,
Into a blood orange evening sky, tasting citrus flavored air
while catching butterflies in your hair,
At the Zambezi river drinking from the waterfalls of Mosi-oa-
Tunya, with your candy yam sweetness and the hips of a
pear ,
You've been dipped in the Sun like black gold radiating
creaminess, like sunbathing in Shea Butter,
As you color summer with
beauty and wonder, under the clouds of Kush, we recline into
the comfort of lovers,
While my kisses on the back of your neck drip into puddles at
the small of back,
Like chocolate prayer beads melting over your curves ,
Lord have mercy, I'll eat watermelon out of your
Lap,
Until you sugarcoat my lips in the honey flow of your
blackberry pie,

Black August

If I'm sinning , I've been forgiven by the Women of Yemen who told me that Lovers are their own Mecca, so make a pilgrimage to your own heart, and I blew the Moon out, Just After Dark....

REVOLUTIONARY LOVE

Up Against the system we Fought and Taught...Sacrificed and RESISTED, Socialist Love Birds and Revolutionaries to the FINISH.... She was my ANGELA DAVIS and I was her GEORGE JACKSON, Comrades in this steady flux of Revolutionary ACTION.... I was Her GUN, She was my TRIGGER and Love was our AMMUNITION.... Her face wasn't made up, because her MIND WAS,..and She never got her nails DONE, Because her hands labored for the people through sweat, tears and BLOOD..... And my hands gripped the neck of the Enemy, watching his eyes pop out his HEAD, I'm a Samurai with a pocket knife, and it's a Bloody Business, trying to keep our Children FED..... Peace was our Dream, but Justice was our AIM, So we mounted it with a Scope and Fired a Shot in the People's NAME..... We ate from the People's stash,...Ran...Hid...Ducked and Fired BACK, Brotha's and Sista's Rebel...give the Pig Hell and Strike the MATCH..... Stop Entertaining, Buck Dancing and BOOT-LICKIN, Snitching and Switching....We Revolutionaries Not Niggas and BITCHES!!!...... She Kisses me at my core, We War for Love, and are So Rich we're POOR, And She's too Real to spend her time shopping in the enemy's department STORES..... It's all about Guns and Butter, If you don't shoot you will MELT, Never FELT, So ALIVE, it's like shooting My NINE between my Woman's THIGHS.... A lot of Pain…..A lot of Blood ....and we are BORN-AGAIN, Up Against the Machine.... to Fight and Die is Honorable, to coward and submit is the worst of SINS.... We Dance to the drum beat of REVOLUTION, The Voice of the People is the Soul of our MUSIC..... The Children's empty Tummies, Allows me no MONEY, Because if they're Hungry, That means I have Too Much...and That aint

FUNNY.... We aint Laughing, Beggin or Asking.....We Jackin and TAKING, Because this is Revolution in the Making,...No Pig in my diet,..I Break The Fast without BACON, Stop Shaking, Don't be Scared....Little Boy....MAN UP!!! You gotta Stand Up, Gotta put your Foot in the Enemy's Ass and make him give the LAND UP...... We don't call each others..."Baby or Boo", WE COMRADES!!!...King and Queen is our THEME, She calls me her Guardian Angel and I call her My WINGS.... She Loves me but Only as much as I Love the People..... and LIKE'WISE, I Like Mine with Brown Eyez and BEAN PIE..... And She gets a Double Scoop of this Dark Chocolate Soul BROTHA, Revolutionary Lovers and Too FREE to do it Under the COVERS..... Just like HUEY said, "We have to Seize The TIME", And don't get caught with your Drawers Down.....Thats Revolutionary SUICIDE.... They aint gonna Kill me in Bed like COMRADE FRED, See we fuck Standing Up...Eat on the Run and Bathe when we CAN.... It's like The TIME said...." This is Jungle LOVE, We use to swing on the monkey bars, Now we're Guerrillas swinging GUNZ.... Aint got No Time to Bling, Guerrillas Lift every Fist and SWING, They put KING to Sleep for having a DREAM.... So you better stay Wide Awake and don't get Sleepy off the WEED, We got Children to Feed and People in NEED.... The Evil Empire is a Vampire, We Bleed for it's GREED..... BACK to BACK with my Woman, We SEE the Enemy COMING, Running and Gunning....Now let me Explain...Just How We DONE IT..... We NEVER Folded,...We Reloaded...Like the MATRIX, You Should've Seen Their FACES....Their Own Blood they TASTED, MuthaFuckin Pig RACIST!!! Keep it Coming you Pig BASTARDS.....You up against Guerrillas and PANTHERS, Liberated Slaves against The SLAVE MASTER(S)....FREEDOM or DEATH!! We Refuse to be CAPTURED!!! It's at that Moment MOST of our People COWERED, Afraid to be

Empowered and take back whats OURS..... But Not US!!!.....We Fought and Died to Show and Prove The Price of FREEDOM and the Value of Our BLOOD, And when your Children ask how they were made Slaves...You shut your Mouth and let them read Our Poem called REVOLUTIONARY LOVE!!!!

Black August

·

www.ingramcontent.com/pod-product-compliance
Lightning Source LLC
LaVergne TN
LVHW041039061225
827171I V00045B/756